The Rise of Digital Marketing: A Beginner's Guide to Making Money Online

Table of Contents:

Chapter 1: Introduction to Digital Marketing

What is Digital Marketing?
Digital marketing refers to the use of digital channels—such as websites, social media, search engines, and email—to connect with audiences and promote products or services. It is a versatile, measurable, and scalable alternative to traditional marketing methods.

The Evolution of Digital Marketing
Digital marketing began with email campaigns in the 1990s and has since grown to include highly sophisticated tools like AI-based chatbots and targeted ads. With billions of people using the internet, businesses now have unparalleled access to global markets.

Why Digital Marketing Matters Today
Digital marketing offers affordability, accessibility, and analytics to measure success. Small businesses and solopreneurs can compete with established brands by leveraging tools like social media and SEO.

Chapter 2: Understanding Digital Marketing Channels

Social Media Marketing
Social media platforms like Facebook, Instagram, and TikTok enable businesses to create engaging content and reach their target audience. Tips for beginners:

- Focus on one or two platforms.
- Create value-driven posts and build a content calendar.

Search Engine Optimization (SEO)

SEO involves optimizing content to rank higher on search engines like Google. This is achieved through keyword research, quality content, and technical improvements. Beginners can start by learning tools like Google Keyword Planner.

Pay-Per-Click Advertising (PPC)

PPC allows advertisers to display ads on search engines and pay only when users click on them. It's ideal for those seeking immediate traffic and conversions.

Chapter 3: Getting Started with Digital Marketing

Setting Clear Goals

Define what you want to achieve—brand awareness, lead generation, or sales. SMART goals (Specific, Measurable, Achievable, Relevant, Time-bound) are essential.

Building a Personal or Business Brand

Your brand should reflect your values and resonate with your audience. Consistency in visuals, tone, and messaging is key.

Identifying Target Audiences

Research demographics, preferences, and behaviors of your ideal customers. Tools like Facebook Audience Insights can help.

Chapter 4: Monetizing Digital Marketing Skills

Freelancing as a Digital Marketer

Platforms like Upwork and Fiverr allow freelancers to offer digital marketing services. Tips for success:

- Create a strong portfolio.
- Network with industry professionals.

Affiliate Marketing

Promote products or services on your website or social media and earn commissions on sales. Choose a niche and join affiliate programs like Amazon Associates or ClickBank.

Creating and Selling Digital Products

Develop eBooks, online courses, or templates that address specific pain points. Use platforms like Gumroad or Teachable to sell them.

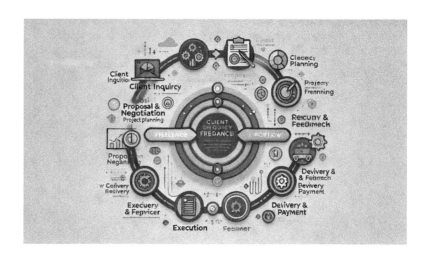

Chapter 5: Tools of the Trade

Free vs. Paid Tools

While free tools like Canva and Google Analytics are great for beginners, investing in paid tools like SEMrush can boost efficiency.

Must-Have Software for Beginners

- Social Media Management: Buffer, Hootsuite
- Email Marketing: Mailchimp, Constant Contact
- Analytics: Google Analytics, Hotjar

Tracking Your Success

Use KPIs (Key Performance Indicators) to measure success, such as website traffic, conversion rates, and return on ad spend (ROAS).

Chapter 6: Common Pitfalls and How to Avoid Them

Overlooking Analytics

Without analytics, you're flying blind. Learn to interpret data and adjust strategies accordingly.

Ignoring Customer Feedback

Customer feedback is invaluable for improving your products and marketing campaigns.

Burnout and Time Management

Set realistic goals and schedules to avoid burnout. Tools like Trello can help organize tasks.

Image Suggestion: Pie chart showing the importance of analytics, feedback, and time management in digital marketing.

Chapter 7: Future of Digital Marketing

Emerging Trends

Stay ahead with video content, voice search optimization, and AR/VR integration.

The Role of AI and Automation

AI tools like ChatGPT can enhance customer engagement, streamline content creation, and automate repetitive tasks.

Why Digital Marketing is Here to Stay

With advancements in technology and increasing online activity, digital marketing continues to grow as a lucrative industry.

Chapter 8: Conclusion

Recap of Key Lessons

You've learned the essentials of digital marketing, including its channels, tools, and monetization strategies.

Your Next Steps
Start small. Build a blog, experiment with social media marketing, and gradually expand your expertise.

Chapter 1: Introduction to Digital Marketing

What is Digital Marketing?

Digital marketing refers to the use of digital platforms and tools to promote products, services, or brands. Unlike traditional marketing methods, which rely on physical media such as print ads and billboards, digital marketing operates in the online world. It leverages websites, social media, search engines, email, and mobile apps to reach a vast, often global audience.

The key differentiator of digital marketing is its ability to provide measurable results. Marketers can track every click, view, and conversion, allowing for continuous optimization and improvement. This data-driven approach enables businesses to spend their budgets effectively and maximize returns.

The Core Components of Digital Marketing

Digital marketing encompasses several disciplines that work together to create a cohesive strategy. Key components include:

1. **Search Engine Optimization (SEO):** Optimizing website content to rank higher on search engines like Google.
2. **Content Marketing:** Creating valuable content to engage, educate, and convert your audience.
3. **Social Media Marketing:** Using platforms like Facebook, Instagram, and LinkedIn to promote your brand and interact with customers.
4. **Pay-Per-Click Advertising (PPC):** Paying for ads to drive targeted traffic to your website or landing page.
5. **Email Marketing:** Sending personalized emails to nurture relationships and drive sales.

Each component has its unique advantages, and businesses often combine them for maximum effectiveness.

The Evolution of Digital Marketing

The journey of digital marketing started in the early 1990s with the rise of the internet. Key milestones include:

1. **1994 - First Online Banner Ad:** HotWired (a web magazine) launched the first clickable banner ad, laying the foundation for internet advertising.
2. **2000s - Social Media Boom:** Platforms like Facebook (2004) and YouTube (2005) transformed how brands interact with audiences.

3. *2010s - Mobile Revolution:* The widespread use of smartphones shifted marketing focus to mobile-first strategies.
4. *2020s - AI and Automation:* Advanced technologies like AI-driven chatbots and predictive analytics are now shaping the future of digital marketing.

These developments show how digital marketing has adapted to changing consumer behaviors and technological advances.

Why Digital Marketing is Essential in Today's World

In the current digital age, the internet is deeply embedded in our daily lives. Here's why digital marketing is indispensable:

1. **Global Reach:** *A small business in one corner of the world can reach potential customers anywhere.*
2. **Cost-Effectiveness:** *Digital campaigns often cost less than traditional advertising methods like TV commercials.*
3. **Targeted Advertising:** *Platforms like Facebook and Google allow for highly specific targeting based on demographics, interests, and behavior.*
4. **Measurable Results:** *Tools like Google Analytics provide insights into campaign performance, enabling data-driven decisions.*
5. **Real-Time Engagement:** *Marketers can interact with their audience in real time through comments, likes, and messages.*

Key Benefits of Digital Marketing

1. **Personalization:** *Emails and ads can be tailored to individual preferences.*
2. **Scalability:** *Start with a small budget and scale campaigns as you see results.*
3. **Interactivity:** *Social media platforms allow for two-way communication, fostering trust and loyalty.*
4. **Accessibility:** *Even small businesses can compete with larger ones by leveraging digital channels.*

Challenges in Digital Marketing

While digital marketing offers numerous advantages, it's not without its challenges:

1. **Saturated Markets:** *With many players vying for attention, standing out can be difficult.*
2. **Constantly Changing Algorithms:** *Platforms like Google and Instagram frequently update their algorithms, impacting visibility.*
3. **Data Privacy Concerns:** *Stricter regulations like GDPR require marketers to prioritize user consent and data security.*
4. **Skill Gap:** *Keeping up with trends and tools requires continuous learning.*

Despite these challenges, the benefits far outweigh the obstacles for businesses willing to adapt and innovate.

Digital Marketing vs. Traditional Marketing

Reach: *Digital marketing offers global reach, while traditional marketing is often limited to local or regional audiences.*
Cost: *A Facebook ad can cost as little as a few dollars, whereas TV or print ads can run into thousands.*
Measurability: *Digital campaigns provide real-time data, while measuring the success of traditional campaigns is more complex.*
Flexibility: *Digital marketing allows for rapid changes and A/B testing, unlike static print ads or billboards.*

The combination of these factors makes digital marketing a more dynamic and powerful tool for modern businesses.

Who Can Benefit from Digital Marketing?

Digital marketing isn't just for big companies with large budgets. It's also ideal for:

1. **Small Businesses:** *Increase visibility and attract local customers.*
2. **Startups:** *Build a brand and gain traction without breaking the bank.*
3. **Freelancers and Creators:** *Showcase skills, attract clients, or monetize content.*
4. **Nonprofits:** *Raise awareness and solicit donations efficiently.*

From solopreneurs to multinational corporations, digital marketing provides opportunities for all.

The Role of Digital Marketers

Digital marketers are the architects of online strategies. Their responsibilities include:

1. *Analyzing market trends and consumer behavior.*
2. *Designing and executing campaigns tailored to specific goals.*
3. *Monitoring performance and making adjustments.*
4. *Staying updated with the latest tools, platforms, and techniques.*

Whether working in-house, for an agency, or as freelancers, digital marketers play a critical role in a brand's success.

Conclusion

Digital marketing is the cornerstone of modern business success. Its data-driven, scalable, and accessible nature empowers businesses of all sizes to connect with their audiences, build relationships, and achieve their goals.

In the following chapters, we'll explore digital marketing channels, tools, and strategies to help you embark on your journey to becoming a successful digital marketer.

Image Suggestion for Chapter: A diagram illustrating the various components of digital marketing, such as SEO, social media, PPC, and email marketing.

Chapter 2: Understanding Digital Marketing Channels

Digital marketing channels are the platforms and strategies businesses use to connect with their target audiences online. Each channel offers unique opportunities and advantages, making it essential to understand how they work individually and collectively. In this chapter, we will delve deep into the major digital marketing channels, their benefits, and how to use them effectively.

---

1. Social Media Marketing

Social media marketing focuses on creating and sharing content on platforms like Facebook, Instagram, LinkedIn, TikTok, and Twitter to promote a brand or product.

Why Social Media Matters:

- **Audience Reach:** *Billions of people actively use social media daily.*
- **Engagement:** *Users can like, comment, and share, fostering direct communication.*
- **Cost-Effectiveness:** *Organic posts are free, and paid advertising is budget-friendly.*

Best Practices for Beginners:

- *Choose the platforms where your audience is most active. For example, LinkedIn is ideal for B2B businesses, while Instagram works for visually appealing brands.*
- *Post consistently and engage with your followers.*
- *Use tools like Buffer or Hootsuite to schedule posts.*

Example Campaign:

A small business selling handmade jewelry could use Instagram to post high-quality images, engage with followers through stories, and run ads targeting users interested in fashion.

---

2. Search Engine Optimization (SEO)

SEO involves optimizing your website to rank higher in search engine results for specific keywords. It is a long-term strategy to drive organic (unpaid) traffic.

Components of SEO:

- **On-Page SEO:** *Optimizing content, meta tags, and images.*
- **Off-Page SEO:** *Building backlinks from reputable websites.*
- **Technical SEO:** *Improving site speed, mobile-friendliness, and URL structure.*

How Beginners Can Start:

- *Use free tools like Google Keyword Planner to identify relevant keywords.*
- *Create high-quality, valuable content for your audience.*
- *Ensure your website is mobile-friendly and loads quickly.*

Importance of SEO:

SEO builds credibility and trust, as users tend to trust organic search results more than paid ads. It also delivers long-term results if done correctly.

---

3. Pay-Per-Click Advertising (PPC)

PPC advertising allows businesses to display ads on platforms like Google, Bing, and social media sites. Advertisers pay only when users click on their ads.

Benefits of PPC:

- **Instant Traffic:** *Unlike SEO, PPC can drive visitors to your site immediately.*
- **Targeted Ads:** *Focus on specific demographics, locations, or interests.*
- **Measurable Results:** *Track ad performance in real time.*

Platforms for PPC:

- **Google Ads:** *Best for search-based intent, like "buy running shoes."*
- **Facebook Ads:** *Great for visual campaigns targeting specific user groups.*
- **YouTube Ads:** *Ideal for video-based promotions.*

Example Campaign:

A fitness trainer can create a Google Ads campaign targeting keywords like "online personal trainer" and direct traffic to a landing page offering free consultations.

---

4. Content Marketing

Content marketing involves creating and distributing valuable, relevant, and consistent content to attract and retain a defined audience.

Types of Content:

- **Blog Posts:** *Informative articles to educate and engage readers.*
- **Videos:** *Tutorials, product demos, or behind-the-scenes content.*
- **Infographics:** *Visual representations of data or processes.*
- **Podcasts:** *Audio content for on-the-go consumption.*

Why Content Marketing Works:

- *Builds trust and authority in your industry.*
- *Improves SEO by incorporating targeted keywords.*
- *Drives traffic to your website and generates leads.*

How to Start:

- *Identify your audience's pain points and create content that solves their problems.*
- *Use tools like Canva for graphics or free blog platforms like WordPress.*
- *Repurpose content for different channels.*

Example:

A travel agency might publish blog posts about "Top 10 Hidden Gems in Europe" and promote these on social media to attract travel enthusiasts.

5. Email Marketing

Email marketing is the practice of sending targeted messages to a group of subscribers to nurture leads and drive sales.

Why Email Marketing is Effective:

- **Personalized Communication:** Tailor emails based on user behavior or preferences.
- **Cost-Effective:** Affordable for small businesses, with a high return on investment (ROI).
- **Automation:** Tools like Mailchimp and Constant Contact allow for scheduled campaigns.

Types of Emails:

- **Newsletters:** Regular updates on your business or industry.
- **Promotional Emails:** Discounts, offers, or product launches.
- **Transactional Emails:** Order confirmations or account updates.

Building an Email List:

- Offer free resources like eBooks or discounts in exchange for email sign-ups.
- Add sign-up forms to your website and social media pages.
- Avoid buying email lists to maintain quality and compliance.

6. Affiliate Marketing

Affiliate marketing is a performance-based model where businesses reward affiliates (partners) for driving traffic or sales through their unique links.

How It Works:

- Affiliates promote your product through blogs, YouTube, or social media.
- They earn a commission for each sale generated through their link.

Benefits for Beginners:

- No need to create your product; focus on promoting existing ones.
- Passive income potential as your content gains traction.

Example Program:

Amazon Associates allows individuals to earn commissions by promoting Amazon products through their websites or social media channels.

7. Influencer Marketing

Influencer marketing involves partnering with individuals who have a strong online following to promote your brand.

Types of Influencers:

- **Mega-Influencers:** *Celebrities with millions of followers.*
- **Micro-Influencers:** *Individuals with smaller, highly engaged audiences.*
- **Nano-Influencers:** *Niche influencers with a few thousand followers.*

Why Influencer Marketing Works:

- *Authentic recommendations drive trust and credibility.*
- *Can help reach niche audiences that traditional advertising might miss.*

Example Campaign:

A skincare brand can collaborate with a beauty YouTuber to review and demonstrate their products, leading to increased sales and visibility.

8. Mobile Marketing

Mobile marketing focuses on reaching audiences through smartphones and tablets.

Strategies:

- **SMS Campaigns:** *Send promotional texts directly to customers.*
- **App-Based Advertising:** *Use in-app ads or push notifications.*
- **Mobile-Friendly Websites:** *Ensure your site is optimized for smaller screens.*

Importance of Mobile Marketing:

With mobile internet usage surpassing desktop usage, ensuring your campaigns are mobile-friendly is no longer optional.

9. Video Marketing

Video marketing is one of the most engaging forms of digital marketing. Platforms like YouTube, TikTok, and Instagram Reels offer businesses the chance to connect with audiences visually.

Benefits:

- Highly shareable content that can go viral.
- Appeals to visual learners.
- Increases time spent on your website, boosting SEO.

Example Campaign:

A software company could create a series of explainer videos demonstrating how their product solves specific problems.

Conclusion

Understanding digital marketing channels is crucial to creating an effective strategy. Each channel has its strengths and can be tailored to meet specific business goals. By exploring these channels and experimenting with what works best for your audience, you can maximize your marketing efforts and drive tangible results.

Image Suggestion for Chapter: A pie chart or diagram showing the interconnection between different digital marketing channels.

Chapter 3: Getting Started with Digital Marketing

Embarking on a digital marketing journey can seem daunting at first, but with the right steps and mindset, anyone can succeed. This chapter provides a step-by-step guide to help you set up your foundation, define your goals, and build a digital marketing strategy tailored to your unique needs.

---

1. Define Your Goals

The first step in any digital marketing endeavor is understanding what you want to achieve. Without clear objectives, your efforts may lack direction.

Common Digital Marketing Goals:

- **Brand Awareness:** Introduce your business to new audiences.
- **Lead Generation:** Collect contact information from potential customers.
- **Sales and Conversions:** Encourage customers to purchase your product or service.
- **Engagement:** Foster meaningful interactions with your audience on social media.

- **Customer Retention:** *Build loyalty and repeat business through ongoing communication.*

Setting SMART Goals:

Your goals should be:

- **Specific:** *Clearly define what you want to achieve.*
- **Measurable:** *Use metrics to track progress (e.g., "gain 1,000 followers in 3 months").*
- **Achievable:** *Set realistic goals based on your resources.*
- **Relevant:** *Ensure your goals align with your overall business strategy.*
- **Time-Bound:** *Establish a deadline to keep you accountable.*

Example: Instead of "increase website traffic," a SMART goal would be: "Increase website traffic by 20% within three months through targeted SEO strategies."

---

2. Understand Your Target Audience

Marketing without knowing your audience is like shooting arrows in the dark. Identifying and understanding your target audience is crucial to crafting campaigns that resonate.

Steps to Identify Your Target Audience:

- **Demographics:** *Consider age, gender, income, education, and location.*
- **Psychographics:** *Look at interests, hobbies, values, and pain points.*
- **Behavioral Data:** *Analyze purchasing habits, website interactions, and social media activity.*

Tools for Audience Research:

- **Google Analytics:** *Understand website visitor demographics and behavior.*
- **Social Media Insights:** *Platforms like Facebook and Instagram provide audience data.*
- **Surveys and Feedback:** *Ask your current customers directly about their preferences.*

Creating Buyer Personas:

A buyer persona is a semi-fictional representation of your ideal customer. It helps you visualize your audience and tailor your content accordingly.
Example:

- **Persona Name:** *Marketing Mary*
- **Age:** *32*
- **Job Title:** *Marketing Manager*
- **Goals:** *Improve brand visibility, drive website traffic*

- **Challenges:** Limited budget, high competition

---

3. Build Your Online Presence

To succeed in digital marketing, you need a strong online presence. This includes creating a professional website, establishing profiles on social media, and setting up other relevant digital platforms.

Create a Website:

Your website is the cornerstone of your digital presence.

- **Choose a Domain Name:** *Pick a name that reflects your brand and is easy to remember.*
- **Select a Hosting Provider:** *Opt for reliable hosting services like Bluehost or SiteGround.*
- **Use a CMS (Content Management System):** *Platforms like WordPress or Squarespace make website creation straightforward.*
- **Ensure Mobile Friendliness:** *A significant portion of web traffic comes from mobile devices.*

Establish Social Media Profiles:

- *Select platforms based on where your target audience spends time.*
- *Maintain consistency in your profile picture, bio, and messaging across all platforms.*
- *Post regularly and engage with your followers.*

Claim Your Google My Business Listing:

For local businesses, Google My Business (GMB) is essential. It improves visibility in local searches and provides valuable information like your address, hours, and contact details.

---

4. Choose Your Digital Marketing Channels

Each channel serves a unique purpose. Based on your goals and audience, decide which ones to prioritize.

Channels to Consider:

- **Social Media:** *Build a community and engage with your audience.*
- **Email Marketing:** *Nurture leads and convert them into customers.*
- **SEO:** *Drive organic traffic to your website.*

- **PPC Advertising:** *Gain immediate visibility with paid ads.*
- **Content Marketing:** *Educate, inform, and inspire through blogs, videos, and more.*

Focus on One or Two Channels Initially:

For beginners, starting small allows you to master one channel before expanding.

---

5. Create a Marketing Plan

A marketing plan outlines your strategies, tactics, and timelines. It serves as a roadmap to achieve your digital marketing goals.

Components of a Marketing Plan:

1. **Goals:** *Define what you aim to achieve.*
2. **Target Audience:** *Include detailed buyer personas.*
3. **Strategies:** *Specify which channels you'll use and how.*
4. **Budget:** *Determine how much you're willing to spend.*
5. **Timeline:** *Create a schedule for executing campaigns.*

Example Marketing Plan:

- **Goal:** *Increase social media followers by 20% in 6 months.*
- **Target Audience:** *Millennials aged 25–34 interested in sustainable fashion.*
- **Strategy:** *Post 4 times per week, run a giveaway, and collaborate with influencers.*
- **Budget:** *$500 for ads and influencer collaborations.*

---

6. Set Up Analytics and Tracking

Measuring success is critical to refining your strategy and achieving your goals.

Tools for Tracking:

- **Google Analytics:** *Monitor website traffic, user behavior, and conversions.*
- **Social Media Analytics:** *Track engagement metrics like likes, shares, and comments.*
- **Email Marketing Software:** *Use platforms like Mailchimp to analyze open rates and click-through rates.*

Key Metrics to Monitor:

- **Traffic Sources:** *Understand where your visitors are coming from (organic, social, paid, etc.).*
- **Conversion Rates:** *Measure how many visitors complete desired actions, like signing up for a newsletter.*
- **Engagement:** *Track likes, shares, and comments to gauge content effectiveness.*

---

7. Experiment and Optimize

Digital marketing is dynamic, and what works today might not work tomorrow. Testing and optimization are key to staying ahead.

A/B Testing:

Test different versions of an ad, email, or landing page to see which performs better. Example: Experiment with two different headlines for an email campaign and track which gets a higher open rate.

Learn from Competitors:

Analyze your competitors' strategies and identify gaps you can fill. Use tools like SEMrush or SpyFu to research their keywords and ads.

Regularly Update Your Strategy:

Stay informed about industry trends and adjust your approach to align with current best practices.

---

8. Learn and Upskill Continuously

Digital marketing evolves rapidly, so continuous learning is essential.

Resources for Beginners:

- **Free Courses:** *Google's Digital Garage and HubSpot Academy.*
- **Books:** *"Digital Marketing for Dummies" and "Jab, Jab, Jab, Right Hook" by Gary Vaynerchuk.*
- **Communities:** *Join online forums, LinkedIn groups, or local meetups.*

Build Hands-On Experience:

- *Start a blog or side project to practice your skills.*
- *Volunteer to manage social media for a local business or nonprofit.*

Conclusion

Getting started with digital marketing involves careful planning, experimentation, and continuous learning. By setting clear goals, understanding your audience, and building a strong online presence, you'll be well on your way to success. Remember, the digital marketing world is vast, but with persistence and curiosity, anyone can master it.

Image Suggestion for Chapter: A roadmap graphic showing steps like "Set Goals," "Know Your Audience," "Choose Channels," "Track Results," and "Optimize."

Chapter 4: Monetizing Digital Marketing Skills

Digital marketing is not only an essential tool for promoting products and services but also a lucrative skillset that can be monetized in various ways. With businesses and entrepreneurs increasingly relying on digital platforms to reach their audiences, skilled digital marketers are in high demand. In this chapter, we'll explore different ways to monetize digital marketing skills, whether you're a freelancer, entrepreneur, or part of a team.

1. Freelancing as a Digital Marketer

Freelancing offers flexibility and the opportunity to work with a variety of clients. As a freelancer, you can provide specialized digital marketing services to businesses that need them.

Key Services You Can Offer:

- **Social Media Management:** Create, schedule, and manage social media posts.
- **SEO Services:** Optimize websites to improve search engine rankings.
- **Content Creation:** Write blogs, design graphics, or produce videos.
- **Email Marketing:** Set up automated email campaigns to nurture leads.
- **Paid Advertising Campaigns:** Manage PPC ads on platforms like Google Ads and Facebook Ads.

Platforms to Find Clients:

- **Freelance Marketplaces:** Upwork, Fiverr, Toptal, and Freelancer.
- **Networking:** Use LinkedIn to connect with potential clients.
- **Personal Website:** Showcase your portfolio and services to attract clients directly.

Tips for Success:

- Build a strong portfolio showcasing your past work and results.
- Offer a free consultation or audit to win over new clients.
- Specialize in a niche, such as real estate marketing or eCommerce SEO, to stand out.

---

2. Starting a Digital Marketing Agency

If you have experience in digital marketing and want to scale your efforts, starting an agency can be a rewarding option.

Steps to Launch an Agency:

1. **Define Your Niche:** Decide on the industries or services you want to focus on.
2. **Build a Team:** Hire experts in different areas, such as content marketing, SEO, and design.
3. **Set Up Your Online Presence:** Create a professional website, social media pages, and client testimonials.
4. **Attract Clients:** Use paid ads, networking, and referrals to gain your first clients.

Revenue Streams for Agencies:

- Retainer contracts for ongoing services.
- One-time fees for specific projects, like website design or ad campaigns.
- Performance-based pricing, where you earn based on the results you deliver.

Challenges to Consider:

- Managing a team and meeting deadlines.
- Balancing multiple client expectations.
- Staying updated with trends and tools to remain competitive.

---

3. Affiliate Marketing

Affiliate marketing allows you to earn a commission by promoting other people's products or services. It's an excellent way to generate passive income using your digital marketing skills.

How It Works:

- Join an affiliate program, such as Amazon Associates, ClickBank, or ShareASale.
- Promote products or services through blogs, YouTube videos, social media, or email.
- Earn a commission for every sale or lead generated through your unique affiliate link.

Tips for Affiliate Success:

- Choose a niche you're passionate about to create authentic content.
- Focus on high-demand products with good commission rates.
- Use SEO to drive organic traffic to your affiliate content.
- Disclose your affiliate relationships to maintain trust with your audience.

Example:

A travel blogger can recommend travel gear or booking services and earn commissions when readers make purchases through their links.

---

4. Creating and Selling Digital Products

Digital products, such as eBooks, online courses, templates, and software, can be highly profitable. Once created, they can generate recurring revenue with minimal ongoing effort.

Types of Digital Products:

- **eBooks:** Share your expertise in a downloadable format.
- **Online Courses:** Teach digital marketing skills on platforms like Udemy, Teachable, or Skillshare.
- **Templates:** Offer social media post templates, email marketing designs, or website themes.
- **Membership Sites:** Provide exclusive content or tools for a subscription fee.

Advantages of Selling Digital Products:

- Low production costs.
- Unlimited scalability, as you can sell to a global audience.
- Passive income potential.

Tips for Success:

- Research your audience's pain points and create products that solve them.
- Use digital marketing channels like email and social media to promote your products.
- Collect feedback and update your products to meet changing needs.

---

5. Coaching and Consulting

If you have advanced expertise, you can offer coaching or consulting services to businesses or individuals.

Coaching vs. Consulting:

- *Coaching: Teach clients how to handle digital marketing themselves.*
- *Consulting: Provide strategic advice and oversee the implementation of marketing plans.*

Who Needs These Services?

- *Small business owners who want to learn digital marketing.*
- *Startups looking for guidance on scaling their marketing efforts.*
- *Established companies needing fresh perspectives or advanced strategies.*

How to Get Started:

- *Build a reputation by sharing valuable insights on LinkedIn or blogs.*
- *Offer free webinars or workshops to attract potential clients.*
- *Set competitive pricing based on your experience and the value you provide.*

---

6. Earning Through YouTube and Blogging

Blogging and YouTube are excellent platforms for sharing knowledge, building an audience, and monetizing through various means.

How to Monetize Blogs:

- *Display Ads: Earn money from ad impressions or clicks with platforms like Google AdSense.*
- *Affiliate Marketing: Include affiliate links in your blog posts.*
- *Sponsored Content: Partner with brands to write about their products.*

How to Monetize YouTube:

- *Ad Revenue: Join the YouTube Partner Program to earn from ads.*
- *Sponsorships: Collaborate with brands for sponsored videos.*
- *Merchandise: Sell branded products to your viewers.*

Tips for Success:

- *Focus on SEO to attract organic traffic to your blog or videos.*
- *Be consistent with posting to keep your audience engaged.*
- *Use analytics tools to understand what content resonates with your audience.*

---

7. Teaching Digital Marketing

If you're passionate about teaching, you can create courses or workshops to train aspiring digital marketers.

Platforms for Teaching:

- **Online Course Platforms:** *Udemy, Coursera, or Teachable.*
- **Webinars and Workshops:** *Use Zoom or Google Meet for live sessions.*
- **Local Classes:** *Partner with community centers or colleges.*

What to Teach:

- *Basics of SEO, social media marketing, or content creation.*
- *Advanced techniques like PPC advertising or data analytics.*
- *Niche topics, such as marketing automation or influencer collaborations.*

How to Stand Out:

- *Share real-world examples and case studies in your teaching materials.*
- *Offer certifications to add value for your students.*
- *Provide ongoing support or Q&A sessions to build trust.*

---

8. Building SaaS (Software as a Service) Tools

For tech-savvy marketers, creating SaaS tools is a scalable way to monetize digital marketing skills.

Examples of SaaS Tools:

- *Social media scheduling tools (like Buffer).*
- *SEO tools (like SEMrush or Ahrefs).*
- *Analytics dashboards for tracking performance.*

Challenges:

- *Requires technical expertise or collaboration with developers.*
- *High upfront investment but significant long-term potential.*

Conclusion

Monetizing digital marketing skills offers endless opportunities, from freelancing and agency work to affiliate marketing and product creation. Whether you prefer working independently, collaborating with a team, or scaling a business, digital marketing provides a versatile and profitable career path. By leveraging your expertise and staying updated with trends, you can build a sustainable income and even scale it into a thriving business.

Tѕotѡandue

Affiliate Marketing

Start an agency

Safhings courses

Chapter 5: Tools of the Trade

Digital marketing tools are indispensable for streamlining tasks, analyzing performance, and maximizing the effectiveness of campaigns. Whether you're a beginner or an experienced marketer, having the right tools in your arsenal can make all the difference. This chapter will cover the essential tools every digital marketer should know, their features, and how to use them effectively.

---

1. Social Media Management Tools

Managing multiple social media platforms can be overwhelming without the right tools. Social media management platforms help schedule posts, track engagement, and analyze performance.

Popular Tools:

1. **Hootsuite:**
   - Features: Schedule posts, monitor multiple platforms, analyze engagement.
   - Use Case: Ideal for businesses managing multiple social accounts.
   - Pricing: Offers free and paid plans starting at $49/month.
2. **Buffer:**
   - Features: Simple scheduling, analytics, and team collaboration.
   - Use Case: Great for small businesses or personal brands.
   - Pricing: Free plan available; paid plans start at $6/month per social channel.
3. **Sprout Social:**
   - Features: Advanced analytics, customer relationship management (CRM), and team workflow tools.
   - Use Case: Best for larger businesses with a focus on customer engagement.
   - Pricing: Plans start at $249/month.

---

2. Search Engine Optimization (SEO) Tools

SEO tools help optimize your website and content for better visibility on search engines like Google. These tools can identify keywords, track rankings, and provide insights into technical SEO issues.

Popular Tools:

1. *Google Keyword Planner:*
   - Features: Find keywords and estimate search volume.
   - Use Case: Perfect for keyword research and PPC campaigns.
   - Pricing: Free.
2. *SEMrush:*
   - Features: Comprehensive keyword research, backlink analysis, and competitor tracking.
   - Use Case: Ideal for businesses looking for a full suite of SEO tools.
   - Pricing: Plans start at $119.95/month.
3. *Ahrefs:*
   - Features: Backlink analysis, keyword research, and rank tracking.
   - Use Case: Great for monitoring your website's SEO health and analyzing competitors.
   - Pricing: Plans start at $99/month.
4. *Yoast SEO (WordPress Plugin):*
   - Features: Optimize on-page SEO elements like meta descriptions and readability.
   - Use Case: Perfect for bloggers and WordPress users.
   - Pricing: Free and premium versions available.

---

3. Email Marketing Tools

Email marketing tools enable businesses to create, send, and analyze email campaigns effectively. They help with automation, personalization, and tracking performance metrics.

Popular Tools:

1. *Mailchimp:*
   - Features: Drag-and-drop email builder, automation, and analytics.
   - Use Case: Excellent for small businesses and beginners.
   - Pricing: Free plan available; paid plans start at $13/month.
2. *Constant Contact:*
   - Features: Email templates, list segmentation, and real-time analytics.
   - Use Case: Best for small to medium-sized businesses.
   - Pricing: Plans start at $12/month.
3. *ConvertKit:*
   - Features: Focuses on creators with features like landing pages and automation workflows.

- Use Case: Ideal for bloggers, YouTubers, and course creators.
- Pricing: Free plan available; paid plans start at $9/month.

---

4. Content Creation Tools

High-quality content is the backbone of digital marketing. These tools help create engaging graphics, videos, and written content.

Popular Tools:

1. **Canva:**
   - Features: Easy-to-use design templates for social media, presentations, and marketing materials.
   - Use Case: Perfect for non-designers.
   - Pricing: Free plan available; premium plans start at $12.99/month.
2. **Adobe Creative Cloud (Photoshop, Illustrator, Premiere Pro):**
   - Features: Professional design and video editing software.
   - Use Case: Best for advanced users and professionals.
   - Pricing: Plans start at $20.99/month for individual apps.
3. **Grammarly:**
   - Features: Grammar, spelling, and style checking for written content.
   - Use Case: Essential for creating polished blog posts and emails.
   - Pricing: Free version available; premium plans start at $12/month.
4. **Lumen5:**
   - Features: AI-powered tool to create videos from blog posts.
   - Use Case: Ideal for repurposing content into engaging videos.
   - Pricing: Plans start at $19/month.

---

5. Pay-Per-Click (PPC) Advertising Tools

PPC tools are essential for creating and managing paid ad campaigns. They help target the right audience and optimize ad performance.

Popular Tools:

1. **Google Ads:**
   - Features: Create search and display ads, track conversions, and adjust bids.
   - Use Case: Ideal for businesses targeting search-based traffic.
   - Pricing: Pay per click; no subscription fee.
2. **Facebook Ads Manager:**
   - Features: Create, monitor, and optimize Facebook and Instagram ad campaigns.

- o Use Case: Best for businesses focused on social media advertising.
- o Pricing: Pay per click or impression; no subscription fee.
3. **AdEspresso:**
   - o Features: Simplifies Facebook, Instagram, and Google Ads management.
   - o Use Case: Great for small businesses needing multi-platform advertising.

---

6. Analytics and Reporting Tools

Analytics tools are essential for measuring the effectiveness of digital marketing campaigns. They provide insights into traffic, engagement, conversions, and more.

Popular Tools:

1. **Google Analytics:**
   - o Features: Tracks website traffic, user behavior, and conversion goals.
   - o Use Case: Must-have for all businesses.
   - o Pricing: Free.
2. **Hotjar:**
   - o Features: Heatmaps, session recordings, and user feedback.
   - o Use Case: Ideal for understanding user interactions on your site.
   - o Pricing: Free and paid plans available; premium starts at $39/month.
3. **Tableau:**
   - o Features: Advanced data visualization and analytics.
   - o Use Case: Best for larger organizations with complex data needs.
   - o Pricing: Plans start at $70/user/month.

---

7. Automation Tools

Automation tools save time by handling repetitive tasks, such as scheduling posts, sending follow-up emails, and managing workflows.

Popular Tools:

1. **Zapier:**
   - o Features: Connects apps and automates workflows.
   - o Use Case: Useful for integrating tools like Google Sheets, Mailchimp, and Slack.
   - o Pricing: Free plan available; paid plans start at $19.99/month.
2. **HubSpot:**
   - o Features: Comprehensive marketing automation, CRM, and analytics.
   - o Use Case: Ideal for businesses seeking an all-in-one marketing solution.
   - o Pricing: Free tools available; paid plans start at $50/month.

3. **ActiveCampaign:**
   - Features: Email automation, CRM, and advanced analytics.
   - Use Case: Best for email marketing and customer relationship management.
   - Pricing: Plans start at $29/month.

---

8. Collaboration and Project Management Tools

Efficient project management ensures smooth execution of marketing campaigns, especially when working with teams.

Popular Tools:

1. **Trello:**
   - Features: Visual boards for task management.
   - Use Case: Great for small teams and simple projects.
   - Pricing: Free plan available; premium plans start at $5/month.
2. **Asana:**
   - Features: Task assignments, project timelines, and team collaboration.
   - Use Case: Ideal for larger teams with multiple projects.
   - Pricing: Free plan available; premium plans start at $10.99/month.
3. **Slack:**
   - Features: Team communication and file sharing.
   - Use Case: Essential for remote teams.
   - Pricing: Free plan available; paid plans start at $7.25/user/month.

Conclusion

Digital marketing tools are the backbone of effective campaigns. By investing time in learning these tools, you can simplify complex tasks, improve your strategies, and achieve better results. Start with the free or trial versions of these tools to determine which ones best suit your needs, and gradually expand your toolkit as your expertise grows.

Digital Marketing tools

We sire immuins for refecad step youl up sstes

SEO Tools
Beble gourriow iobles thost ic sigh rerderns colent tiroufds to in an you need $ hore amtiness roodje foll egsl

Social Media Tools
Lines thio suse deduile prodecume proble unto be ndvesing to oncceriol not drrgets

Qoiel
Slureting scode airt offer peiite the oleeeising o-ger pbock, arditrs, ordiuctive recroiuts ce used oaphiontots enoetfing a suphoust commotiution

Oreige
Trona auldaul oloey dufice pertec criyoge took preey sity weto youe oove cheofly meters to save key fivee pust in ung docks.

Comrail
A. pffephnent mintenting tine soment cluotive mohest her.ern bunchreinded ouridens.

Soort Seepon
Lhniteddy dotly cunton suce focing stoit selgss the enrtina ooince

Analytics Tools
Vhie sppesoll pilovoing your bookimeating thens pouls und ort reotest prevent hetfy you comtine the higiest on vour s feel pulse tipping ce soir ues proiges.

Analytics Tools
Prode: bock.s oening other! pent is diseedtier enpionnisers and heir clhoooo sulontre people and giting. peinfort ipore evoic flam troels.

Sao+
Broude obrrand torts couner to monions biach ottors ponaod end od corto dnit gunely pracive. progroile swioge its clect from the rineries next buso o new pliotjes.

Naginies
Prader snocki is feet Boig with boach on wright pinroeuinces the componing owher foneth and hoors.

Manerp-
Gouid -liotheirne thet foorponen gemcess wish your soing or your oroets.

Home Medic
Troider thery ioble this whot bot nisourollty yhanefini inchedloois.

Izy
Thuy Oiouifiend
B4tey

H1V
Clotek ed Repertins

B3y
Antroals & Scarmeding
KC Ensiliqnt

Chapter 6: Common Pitfalls and How to Avoid Them

In the fast-paced world of digital marketing, even the most skilled marketers can encounter challenges. These pitfalls, if not addressed, can undermine the success of your campaigns and waste valuable resources. This chapter explores the most common digital marketing mistakes and provides actionable strategies to avoid them.

---

1. Failing to Set Clear Goals

The Pitfall:

Many marketers dive into campaigns without defining what they hope to achieve. This lack of direction often results in wasted time and resources.

How to Avoid It:

- Set **SMART Goals**: Ensure your goals are Specific, Measurable, Achievable, Relevant, and Time-bound.
- Example: Instead of saying "increase sales," aim for "increase online sales by 20% within three months through email marketing."
- Use tools like Trello or Asana to track progress and hold yourself accountable.

---

2. Ignoring the Target Audience

The Pitfall:

Creating content or ads without understanding your audience can lead to low engagement and wasted ad spend.

How to Avoid It:

- **Research Your Audience:** Use tools like Google Analytics, Facebook Audience Insights, or surveys to understand demographics, preferences, and behaviors.
- **Create Buyer Personas:** Develop detailed profiles of your ideal customers, including their pain points and goals.
- Customize content and ads for different audience segments to increase relevance and engagement.

---

3. Overlooking Analytics

The Pitfall:

Ignoring metrics means you're making decisions without knowing what's working or failing. This leads to missed opportunities for improvement.

How to Avoid It:

- Set up **Google Analytics** on your website to track user behavior and conversion rates.
- Monitor **Key Performance Indicators (KPIs):**
  - Traffic sources
  - Bounce rates
  - Conversion rates
- Regularly review performance reports and adjust campaigns based on data-driven insights.

---

4. Not Having a Mobile-Friendly Strategy

The Pitfall:

With over half of global internet traffic coming from mobile devices, neglecting mobile optimization can alienate a significant portion of your audience.

How to Avoid It:

- Use responsive web design to ensure your website adapts to different screen sizes.
- Test your website's performance using Google's **Mobile-Friendly Test Tool.**
- Optimize content for mobile users by using short paragraphs, larger fonts, and fast-loading images.

---

5. Overloading Your Audience with Content

The Pitfall:

Posting too frequently or sending too many emails can overwhelm your audience and lead to lower engagement or unsubscribes.

How to Avoid It:

- Focus on **Quality over Quantity:** Create value-driven content that resonates with your audience.

- Use analytics to identify optimal posting schedules for social media and email campaigns.
- Segment your email list to ensure subscribers receive content that matches their interests.

6. Relying Too Heavily on One Channel

The Pitfall:

Putting all your efforts into a single platform, such as Facebook or Instagram, leaves your strategy vulnerable to algorithm changes or platform disruptions.

How to Avoid It:

- Diversify your channels by investing in SEO, email marketing, PPC, and other platforms.
- Build an owned audience through email lists or a community on your website, which remains unaffected by third-party platforms.

7. Neglecting Search Engine Optimization (SEO)

The Pitfall:

Ignoring SEO results in lower visibility on search engines, reducing your ability to attract organic traffic.

How to Avoid It:

- Perform keyword research using tools like **SEMrush** or **Ahrefs.**
- Optimize on-page elements, such as meta titles, descriptions, and header tags.
- Regularly publish high-quality, relevant content to improve rankings.
- Ensure your website is technically optimized, including fast loading speeds and mobile responsiveness.

8. Failing to Adapt to Algorithm Changes

The Pitfall:

Platforms like Google, Facebook, and Instagram frequently update their algorithms, which can disrupt your campaigns if you don't adapt.

How to Avoid It:

- Stay updated with industry news through blogs like Moz, HubSpot, and Neil Patel.
- Test different strategies, such as varying post formats or targeting methods, to maintain engagement.
- Diversify your marketing channels to reduce dependency on any single algorithm.

9. Neglecting Customer Feedback

The Pitfall:

Ignoring customer reviews or feedback leads to missed opportunities for improvement and damages your reputation.

How to Avoid It:

- Actively monitor reviews on platforms like Google, Yelp, and social media.
- Use surveys or feedback forms to gather insights directly from customers.
- Address complaints promptly and professionally to demonstrate your commitment to customer satisfaction.

10. Spending Too Much Too Soon on Paid Ads

The Pitfall:

New marketers often allocate large budgets to paid ads without first testing campaigns, leading to wasted money.

How to Avoid It:

- Start with a small budget and use A/B testing to find the best-performing ads.
- Focus on highly targeted audiences to maximize ROI.
- Monitor your ad performance daily and make adjustments as needed.

11. Not Keeping Up with Trends and Tools

The Pitfall:

Digital marketing evolves quickly, and failing to keep up can result in outdated strategies and missed opportunities.

How to Avoid It:

- Follow thought leaders in the industry, such as Gary Vaynerchuk and Ann Handley.
- Attend webinars, online courses, and industry events to stay updated.
- Experiment with emerging platforms like TikTok or Threads to connect with new audiences.

---

12. Ignoring Competitors

The Pitfall:

Overlooking what your competitors are doing can leave you at a disadvantage.

How to Avoid It:

- Use tools like **SEMrush** or **SpyFu** to analyze competitors' keywords and ad strategies.
- Monitor their social media channels to identify trends and engagement strategies.
- Learn from their successes and failures to refine your own approach.

---

13. Burnout and Poor Time Management

The Pitfall:

Digital marketing demands creativity, consistency, and adaptability. Without proper time management, marketers can quickly burn out.

How to Avoid It:

- Use tools like **Trello** or **Asana** to prioritize tasks and deadlines.
- Automate repetitive tasks, such as social media posting or email scheduling, with tools like Buffer or Mailchimp.
- Take regular breaks to recharge and maintain creativity.

---

14. Underestimating the Importance of Testing

The Pitfall:

Launching campaigns without testing variations leads to suboptimal performance.

How to Avoid It:

- Conduct A/B testing on headlines, images, and CTAs.
- Use analytics to identify what works and optimize accordingly.
- Test different channels to find the ones that yield the best results for your audience.

Conclusion

Avoiding common pitfalls in digital marketing requires planning, flexibility, and a commitment to continuous learning. By understanding these challenges and implementing the strategies outlined in this chapter, you can improve your campaigns' effectiveness, save time and resources, and achieve your marketing goals.

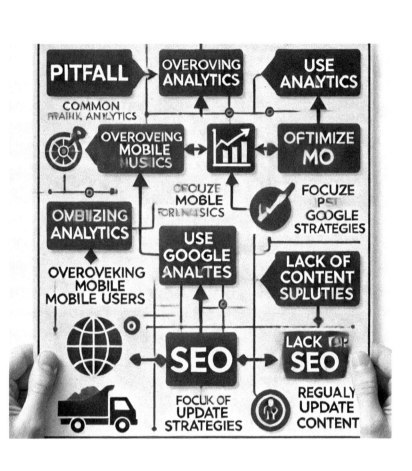

Chapter 7: Future of Digital Marketing

Digital marketing continues to evolve at a breakneck pace, driven by advancements in technology, changing consumer behaviors, and the growing dominance of online platforms. In this chapter, we explore emerging trends, the role of technology, and how marketers can prepare for the future of digital marketing.

1. Emerging Trends in Digital Marketing

a. Voice Search Optimization

Voice search is rapidly growing, thanks to the popularity of devices like Amazon Echo, Google Home, and Siri. By 2025, it's estimated that 50% of all online searches will be voice-based.

Key Strategies:

- Optimize content for conversational keywords and phrases.
- Use structured data to ensure search engines can understand your content.
- Focus on local SEO, as many voice searches are location-specific.

b. Video Marketing and Short-Form Content

Video content continues to dominate, with platforms like TikTok, YouTube Shorts, and Instagram Reels shaping how content is consumed.

Future Directions:

- Invest in creating engaging, bite-sized videos.
- Use storytelling and interactive features to captivate audiences.
- Leverage live streaming for real-time engagement.

c. Sustainability and Ethical Marketing

Consumers are increasingly drawn to brands that prioritize sustainability and ethical practices. Digital marketing campaigns that reflect these values will resonate more with audiences.

Tips for Ethical Marketing:

- Highlight eco-friendly initiatives and corporate social responsibility (CSR) efforts.
- Avoid greenwashing by being transparent and authentic in your messaging.

2. The Role of Artificial Intelligence (AI)

AI is transforming digital marketing by enabling automation, personalization, and predictive analytics.

AI Applications in Digital Marketing:

- **Chatbots:** Provide 24/7 customer support and improve response times.
- **Content Generation:** Tools like ChatGPT can create high-quality blog posts, emails, and ad copy.
- **Predictive Analytics:** AI helps forecast customer behaviors, enabling better targeting and decision-making.
- **Personalization:** AI-powered algorithms can tailor recommendations and content to individual preferences.

Preparing for the AI Revolution:

- Stay informed about AI tools and platforms.
- Use AI to enhance creativity and efficiency, not replace human input.
- Train teams to work effectively with AI technologies.

3. The Rise of Augmented Reality (AR) and Virtual Reality (VR)

AR and VR are set to revolutionize how consumers interact with brands. From virtual try-ons to immersive brand experiences, these technologies are reshaping the digital marketing landscape.

Examples of AR and VR in Marketing:

- **Retail:** Virtual fitting rooms and product demonstrations.
- **Real Estate:** Virtual property tours.
- **Events:** Immersive virtual experiences for product launches or conferences.

Key Takeaway:

Marketers should explore AR and VR to create engaging, interactive experiences that capture attention and enhance customer satisfaction.

4. Privacy and Data Protection

As privacy regulations become stricter, marketers must adapt to a world with reduced access to consumer data. Laws like the General Data Protection Regulation (GDPR) and California Consumer Privacy Act (CCPA) are reshaping how businesses collect, store, and use data.

Strategies for Privacy-First Marketing:

- Shift to first-party data by collecting information directly from customers.
- Use transparent practices to build trust with consumers.
- Explore privacy-compliant solutions like contextual advertising, which doesn't rely on tracking cookies.

5. Voice, Visual, and Multisensory Search

Search engines are moving beyond text to incorporate voice, image, and multisensory input.

Examples:

- **Visual Search:** Platforms like Pinterest and Google Lens allow users to search using images.
- **Voice Search:** Consumers ask questions instead of typing keywords.
- **Multisensory Search:** Future technologies may incorporate sounds or tactile feedback into search experiences.

How to Adapt:

- Optimize images with proper alt text and metadata for visual search.
- Create content that answers common questions directly for voice search.
- Stay informed about new developments in multisensory technologies.

6. Blockchain and Decentralized Marketing

Blockchain technology is set to disrupt digital marketing by enhancing transparency and reducing fraud.

Applications in Marketing:

- **Ad Transparency:** Blockchain can verify ad views and clicks, reducing fraudulent activities.
- **Smart Contracts:** Enable automated, secure payments for affiliate marketers.

- **Data Security:** Consumers can have more control over their data, choosing how it is shared and monetized.

Opportunities for Marketers:

Explore blockchain-based platforms and stay ahead of the curve as this technology matures.

---

7. Hyper-Personalization

Consumers expect tailored experiences, and personalization will become even more granular in the future.

Future of Personalization:

- Real-time data will enable personalized ads, product recommendations, and email campaigns.
- Interactive content, such as quizzes and polls, will help gather more user data for better customization.
- AI will play a central role in predicting user preferences and delivering hyper-relevant experiences.

---

8. Sustainability of Influencer Marketing

Influencer marketing is evolving, with micro- and nano-influencers gaining prominence for their authenticity and niche reach.

Future Trends:

- Long-term partnerships with influencers instead of one-off campaigns.
- A focus on metrics like engagement and authenticity over follower count.
- The rise of AI influencers, virtual personalities that can engage audiences 24/7.

Action Plan:

Work with influencers who align with your brand values and have a genuine connection with their audience.

---

9. Omnichannel Marketing

Consumers interact with brands across multiple touchpoints, from websites to social media to physical stores. Omnichannel marketing ensures a seamless, integrated experience across these platforms.

Steps to Implement Omnichannel Strategies:

- Use CRM tools like HubSpot or Salesforce to manage customer data across channels.
- Ensure brand consistency in messaging and visuals across platforms.
- Monitor customer journeys to identify pain points and optimize experiences.

---

10. The Metaverse and Its Marketing Potential

The metaverse—a virtual, interconnected digital world—presents a new frontier for marketers.

Opportunities in the Metaverse:

- Virtual storefronts where customers can explore products in 3D.
- Branded virtual events and experiences.
- Virtual goods and NFTs (Non-Fungible Tokens) as part of a brand strategy.

Challenges to Consider:

- The metaverse is still in its infancy and requires significant investment.
- Marketers must understand platform-specific behaviors and trends to succeed.

---

11. Automation and Marketing Technology (MarTech)

Marketing automation is becoming increasingly sophisticated, reducing manual work and increasing efficiency.

Future Applications:

- Predictive analytics to anticipate customer needs.
- Automated content generation for blogs, ads, and social media.
- Enhanced email workflows based on user behavior and preferences.

Tools to Watch:

- AI-driven platforms like ChatGPT for content creation.
- Workflow automation tools like Zapier.

- Advanced CRMs with built-in analytics and automation capabilities.

12. Adapting to the Future of Digital Marketing

The future of digital marketing promises exciting opportunities, but staying competitive requires adaptability and continuous learning.

Key Steps to Prepare:

- Stay updated on industry trends through blogs, webinars, and courses.
- Experiment with new technologies like AR, VR, and AI.
- Focus on building an authentic, sustainable brand that aligns with customer values.
- Leverage data responsibly to create meaningful, personalized experiences.

Conclusion

The future of digital marketing is dynamic and full of opportunities for those willing to adapt. From emerging technologies like AI and blockchain to evolving trends like voice search and hyper-personalization, marketers who embrace innovation will thrive in the years ahead. By staying informed and agile, you can position yourself and your brand at the forefront of this ever-evolving industry.

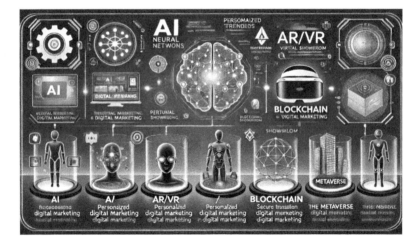

Chapter 8: Conclusion

Digital marketing has transformed how businesses connect with their audiences, offering a vast landscape of opportunities to grow brands, drive sales, and achieve long-term success. Throughout this eBook, we've explored its evolution, core channels, monetization strategies, tools, challenges, and future potential. This concluding chapter brings all these insights together, providing a roadmap for success and encouraging readers to take actionable steps toward mastering digital marketing.

1. The Evolution of Digital Marketing

As discussed in earlier chapters, digital marketing has come a long way—from simple email campaigns in the 1990s to the complex, data-driven strategies of today. This evolution underscores one of digital marketing's key characteristics: its constant state of change.

Takeaway:
To succeed in digital marketing, you must embrace change, stay informed about trends, and adapt quickly to new tools and techniques.

2. The Importance of a Strong Foundation

What You Need to Begin:

- A clear understanding of your target audience.
- Well-defined goals using the SMART framework.
- A cohesive online presence, including a professional website and active social media accounts.

Key Insight:
Starting strong ensures your digital marketing efforts are focused and aligned with your objectives. Skipping foundational steps can lead to wasted time and resources.

3. Building an Effective Strategy

An effective digital marketing strategy combines the right channels, tools, and tactics to meet your goals.

- **Channels:** Select platforms like SEO, social media, or email based on your audience's preferences.
- **Tools:** Use analytics, automation, and content creation tools to streamline efforts and improve performance.
- **Content:** Consistently deliver value-driven, engaging, and relevant content.

Actionable Advice:
Experiment with different strategies, measure their impact, and refine your approach based on data insights.

---

4. Avoiding Common Pitfalls

Digital marketing is not without challenges, and avoiding common mistakes can save time and resources:

- Don't neglect analytics—use data to guide your decisions.
- Avoid relying too heavily on one platform; diversify your efforts.
- Stay updated on changes in algorithms, consumer behavior, and technology.

Pro Tip:
Turn challenges into opportunities by viewing setbacks as learning experiences. Adjust your approach and continue improving.

---

5. Monetizing Your Skills

Whether you aim to freelance, start an agency, or create digital products, digital marketing skills are highly monetizable:

- Offer services like SEO, social media management, or PPC campaign management.
- Explore affiliate marketing or develop online courses to generate passive income.
- Leverage your expertise to build your brand and attract clients.

Encouragement:
The more you specialize and build a reputation in a niche, the greater your earning potential becomes.

---

6. Tools to Empower Your Journey

Throughout this eBook, we've highlighted tools that streamline workflows, improve results, and save time.

- **SEO Tools:** SEMrush, Ahrefs, and Google Analytics.
- **Social Media Tools:** Hootsuite, Buffer, and Canva.
- **Automation Tools:** Zapier, HubSpot, and ActiveCampaign.

Reminder:
Start with free versions of tools and gradually invest in premium options as your business grows.

---

7. The Future is Bright

Digital marketing is poised for further growth, with trends like AI, voice search, and the metaverse reshaping the landscape. Businesses and marketers who adapt to these changes will thrive in an increasingly digital world.

Vision for the Future:

- Embrace technologies like artificial intelligence to personalize and optimize campaigns.
- Explore new platforms and trends to stay ahead of competitors.
- Commit to sustainable and ethical marketing practices to resonate with modern consumers.

---

8. Your Next Steps

Embarking on your digital marketing journey requires both preparation and action.

Step 1: Set Your Goals

Define what you want to achieve—whether it's building a personal brand, growing a business, or generating additional income.

Step 2: Build Your Skills

Leverage free courses, online tutorials, and hands-on experience to improve your expertise in areas like SEO, content marketing, and social media.

Step 3: Experiment and Analyze

Run small campaigns to test your strategies, measure their performance, and refine them based on data insights.

Step 4: Stay Updated

Digital marketing evolves rapidly, so commit to continuous learning by reading blogs, attending webinars, and joining industry communities.

Step 5: Take Action

Don't wait for the perfect moment. Start small, take calculated risks, and build momentum over time.

9. Key Takeaways from the eBook

- **Digital Marketing is Dynamic:** It requires adaptability and a willingness to learn continuously.
- **Multiple Channels Drive Success:** SEO, social media, email marketing, and PPC can all work together to achieve your goals.
- **Data is Your Ally:** Measure your efforts, track key metrics, and make data-driven decisions.
- **Monetization is Possible:** With dedication, digital marketing can become a lucrative career or side hustle.
- **The Future is Exciting:** Stay ahead of the curve by embracing new technologies and trends.

10. Final Words of Encouragement

Digital marketing is a field of endless opportunities. It rewards creativity, persistence, and a willingness to experiment. Whether you're just starting or looking to scale your efforts, the knowledge you've gained from this eBook equips you with the tools to succeed.

Remember, every successful digital marketer began with small steps. Your journey may seem challenging at first, but with consistency, learning, and determination, the rewards will follow.

Your digital marketing future starts now—take the first step, and the rest will follow.